SURVIVING
HIGH SCHOOL

ESSENTIAL TOOLS to **PREPARE YOU** for the **ROAD AHEAD**

A+

Authentic

Surviving High School
Copyright © 2013
Sharon Witt

Cover design by e210.com

Unless otherwise indicated, Scripture taken from the The Message by
Eugene Peterson, copyright 1993, 1994, 1995, 2000, 2001, 2002. Used
by permission of NavPress Publishing Group.
All rights reserved.

Published by Authentic Publishers
188 Front Street, Suite 116-44
Franklin, TN 37064

Authentic Publishers is a division of
Authentic Media, Inc.

Printed in the United States of America

Library of Congress Cataloging-in-Publication Data

Witt, Sharon
      Surviving High School : Essential tools to prepare you for the road
ahead / Sharon Witt
        p. cm.

ISBN 978-1-78078-108-2
    978-1-78078-208-9 (e-book)

Printed in the United States of America
21 20 19 18 17 16 15 14 13   1 2 3 4 5 6 7 8 9 10 11 12

inside

introduction

part 1 a new world, high school

part 2 getting right on the inside

part 3 getting the most out of high school

part 4 help is at hand

introduction
the journey starts here

for those of you who don't just cruise
(that is, almost everyone!)

High school's different for everyone.

For a (very) few, it's a breeze — few hassles and smooth sailing.

But let's be real... for most teens, it takes adjusting. You've got a lot to get a handle on in a short space of time.

Fun? *Yes.*

All the time? *No.*

But can it be fulfilling? *Absolutely!*

High school years can seem very long and fraught with many troubles and stresses. So wherever you are right now with your journey into high school — whether you are about to leave middle school and begin your high school journey or you're already halfway through, remember this important point: Many millions of people have indeed not only survived, but have thrived through high school over the years! They have come through the other end better prepared for life, and have made some awesome friends along the way!

Generally speaking, you will spend four years in high school (*if you are coming from a junior high that includes 9th grade, then it will only be three years*), so that is a very small percentage of your entire life!

It may seem like *forever* all the time, but honestly, before you can blink, you'll be out in the workforce and living life on a much grander scale. So be positive. Remember high school is not the *be all and end all*. In most places, you've got to go. It's compulsory, so why not just go ahead and give the experience your best!

I have been teaching first-year high school students for the better part of 20 years, and I must say, it is an absolute privilege and great fun (*most of the time*). So I hope that the advice and stories in this book will help you get through these years even better.

Right now, you might be getting ready to leave middle school and head off to the big leagues. Or it might have already started and you're wanting some advice on managing the first years of this new adventure. Whatever your age and level of schooling right now, I've written this for you.

Enjoy this book! And enjoy high school!

Sharon

PART 1

A+

a new world, high school

why high school?

and do I really have to *like* anyone there?

"So, what is the point of high school?" I hear you say. Good question, and one that is often asked by exasperated and stressed-out students across the nation. If you think that high school is invented purely to keep you out of the house during the daytime, you're wrong. It's not some conspiracy for parents to get out of baby-sitting!

There are actually so many reasons why high school should be a valuable experience. Sure, you may not realize all of those good points until you're an adult. But then again, you might get a different view after reading this book. You may even enjoy your time in high school! Stranger things have happened.

relationships

One of the greatest benefits of high school is how it can help you hone your social skills. These skills will help you relate to a variety of different people and personalities, both of your own age group and with adults — like teachers, for example! That's a good thing, and extremely helpful when you go into college or the workforce. In that adult world, you'll need the skills to relate to a wide range of people.

Now, you can't be expected to like everyone. That would be boring. And it's not even possible. But getting along with people takes basic tolerance. In short, you do need to learn to cope with other people beyond a handshake or nod of the head. It isn't always easy, but it can be one of the best lessons learned during your high school years.

commitment — seeing tasks through!

Another one of the benefits that can come from high school is the lessons learned from commitment — finishing something you started. This might be completing a science research assignment or attending a school sports carnival and running the mile, even when you don't feel like it. Maybe you joined Student Council at the beginning of the year, and now no longer feel like giving up your lunchtime once a week. Seeing your commitment through to the remainder of the year demonstrates your true character, and shows that you are capable of seeing a commitment through, even when you don't feel like participating.

organization

Learning to be an organized person during high school could perhaps be one of the major benefits of school life. With greater responsibility expected of you in your high school years, you will need to develop your own organizational habits — what works best for you, in order to see your commitments through, such as homework, studying, and completing assignments.

Many of these organizational skills — practicing your time management, study skills, presentation of work, and completing assignments — will prepare you well for college or working in an environment where basic skills are required. Whether you enter a trade, go on to college, or enter the workforce straight from high school, basic organization skills will be a necessity.

"The whole purpose of education is to
turn mirrors into windows."

Sydney J. Harris

---

changes, changes, and more changes

now what corridor did I just walk down?

"I am always ready to learn although I do not always like being taught."

Winston Churchill

One of the first things you'll notice is the size of the place! Often, high school is much larger than what you're used to. Middle school was like a small village. Now you've moved into a big town!

There are more corridors to get lost in – at least in the first week of classes! But don't worry. You'll soon learn your way around and it won't seem so scary.

all these subjects!

One thing you'll already be used to is having many subjects offered and classes to attend. Just like in middle school, your lessons will be run by different teachers. You will have a separate folder and workbooks for each subject, as well as many more textbooks to keep organized. Even if you're familiar with this system, it may seem quite stressful at first; but there are many tips that I'll share later in the book that will help you keep on top of all these books.

back to the bottom

Many teens are also very concerned by the change of status when beginning high school. While you're the older one in the final year of middle school — part of the most experienced group in the school — you feel like you go to the bottom again when entering the high school level! There are three other year levels older than you now, and that can seem more than a little overwhelming. But try to remember that you are never alone, and that you'll only be the new kids on the block for around 10 months. Believe me, the time will really, *really* fly.

new school, new faces

Your peer group or friendship groups can also be a big source of change during high school. Even though your experience might be to enter high school with some of your middle school friends, there are many more students starting at your high school who you don't know. There can often be big changes to friendship groups as a result of new people entering the mix.

wait 'til you get home

Finally, one of the biggest changes that many adolescents experience (and stresses them before they even begin) is that of homework. Yes, there is that dreaded word. We'll talk about this in more detail later, but homework is just a necessary part of high school as you become a more responsible and mature student. For many students, they don't really begin to tackle homework until they start middle school, and even then some slack off and let themselves down. Homework in high school can be even more demanding,

tip time
getting the most out of high school!

get to know other people and include them in your peer group. everyone wins when you help your group to grow!

but don't let that discourage you. Later on, I have some helpful tips on how to tackle your workload.

The best news of all is that the journey into and through high school doesn't have to be a lonely one. In fact, you'll find yourself becoming a more capable and strong person as you go along.

the structure of high school

checking out the lineup

"It isn't how much you learn — it's how much you learn and use."

James Rohn

There are many different types and styles of high schools, just as there are many different personalities and needs of teens.

Firstly, there are public and privately run high schools. Public high schools are basically run by government departments. They decide what is taught and what facilities are available at the school. They rely on taxes paid by parents to provide much-needed funds to keep a school running. Generally speaking, you are most likely to attend a public high school close to where you live, as schools are usually zoned to accommodate local children. Sometimes, you can apply to a public high school that is out of your immediate local area, especially if it has a specific program that is not offered in your local school.

Public high schools have come a long way, and most offer excellent facilities and subject areas. There is no reason you cannot receive the best education in a public school any more than in a private high school.

Private high schools are funded differently from public high schools, and generally rely on school fees that are paid by parents, with some additional funding from private donors, alumni, etc. Private schools charge parents school fees that help to pay teachers' wages, provide school materials and facilities, and all the other expenses that come with running a high school.

Some school fees can be quite high in private schools, but that doesn't always make it the best school.

It's important to note, however, that whether you attend a private or a public high school, you should still have the same opportunities available to any other student. School can be anything and everything you make of it, and it's up to you to seize whatever opportunities you can. Programs, subjects and resources may be very similar in both public and private schools, so it can often come down to a personal decision by parents and students. For example, some private high schools run specifically religious-based programs which might best suit a family's core religious beliefs and values.

Some private schools actually run from the first year (for example, from elementary school) right up to the final year of high school. If you are attending a school such as this, you'll probably be on the same site for both middle school and high school. That certainly makes things easier when graduating from 8th grade — having quite a settled peer group and friendships.

Some high schools are actually structured as same-sex schools. That just means it's an all-girls or all-boys school. For some adolescents, this works better, as they don't have the added distraction of having students of the opposite sex in their classes. It also means that the school can be more flexible in the curriculum when offering courses that especially cater for one of the sexes specifically.

Whether you attend a private or a public high school, you should still have the same opportunities available to any other student.

There are many other examples of different types of high schools. Technical schools focus on more practical subjects such as woodwork and metal work, while there are some high schools (often called "magnet" schools) that have a more specific focus on sports or arts, such as drama and music.

But wherever you end up going for high school, just remember — your experience will be yours, and entirely dependent on what you make of it and the opportunities that you take. So whichever school you attend, or will attend in the future, use this experience to your benefit and make the most of it!

orientation

finding your way around

*"Learning is not attained by chance, it must be sought for
with ardor and attended to with diligence."*

Abigail Adams

I'm a teacher. But I don't know everything, of course!
In fact, I like to hear what students actually think. One of the
questions I ask is a big one — "What are you most worried about
with high school?"

The answers are usually along the lines of, "getting around
the school," or, "finding my way to Mr. Smith's class." It's all
mostly about basic navigation to start with.

The good news here is that there are many other students in
exactly the same boat as you. Many students won't know where
everything is when they kick off high school, or where they are
supposed to be at each hour of the day. You are certainly not
expected to know your way around the whole school from the
very first day, so don't worry.

Almost all high schools have at least one orientation day
prior to new students starting their first year. In fact, some
schools I know of actually have several scheduled orientation
sessions so the students have a few opportunities to get to know
the school and other students. Most schools also offer parent
and student information evenings leading up to the start of high
school. They're a great idea, covering schedules, subjects,
homework, and other school information. If you happen to miss
an orientation session, make sure you ask Mom or Dad to grab
information from the school or have it sent to your home.

During orientation days, you most likely meet your teachers and have a tour of the school grounds to familiarize yourself with where your classes will be held and what facilities are available. You might also receive useful information on these days about sports or other groups you could join during high school. You also find out important transportation information and get the lowdown on cafeteria menus and hours of operation.

year level coordinator, advisor

You most likely get a teacher or counselor assigned to your class or year level who is responsible for guiding you during the transitional weeks. They are the one to approach should you have any questions. This person may be known as the Year Level Coordinator, Home Room Teacher, School Counselor, or even Pastoral Care Teacher. Whatever the title, make sure you identify who your 'go to' teacher is so that you can get help when things get confusing or overwhelming.

finding your way around

You should be given a map of the high school at some stage during the orientation process. Make sure you take the time to familiarize yourself with where your main classes are held. It might also be helpful to use a highlighter pen to show where you need to be for each class. Classrooms are often named by their building block and then classroom number, e.g. C16 or D2. You'll soon work out which rooms and buildings you need to be in.

schedule

During orientation, you should receive a schedule for your different school subjects and teachers. No, don't freak out here!

When you first see your schedule with all the different subjects, times and room numbers, it can seem pretty overwhelming, not to mention confusing. But be reassured that it doesn't take long before your schedule seems like second nature. Some high schools run their schedules on a two-week cycle, which means that week one is different from week two, and then the process repeats itself again. Other schools run with the same schedule each week. Subjects are usually taught in blocks known commonly as "periods," or lessons, and run for between 40-70 minutes.

tip time

getting the most out of high school!

be reassured... it doesn't take long before your schedule seems like second nature.

uniform

Sometimes high schools have some sort of "uniform," plus gym clothes or a sports uniform. Many schools simply have a dress code that you must follow. The school uniform could be as simple as school created or approved t-shirts right up to a pre-scribed outfit. If this is the case, it's important to make sure you have all the right parts of your uniform well before you begin the new school year. Sometimes, schools will have a secondhand clothing option and a uniform shop that you can purchase items from. Make sure you get your school shoes early in the summer before you begin, so you can wear them around the house a bit.

transportation

Some students may already use school–provided transportation (like the school bus) to get to and from their high school; some may even use public transportation. And of course many walk, drive, or catch a ride with parents or friends. If you are using public transportation to get to school, it would be a good idea to have a practice run or two during the summer before you start school. At the very least, you should familiarize yourself with the bus schedule and make an extra copy to keep in your school bag or planner.

prospectus

Finally, most schools produce a prospectus, or brochure, for the first year of high school. You should be able to pick one up from the school office if you don't receive one as part of your orientation package. These booklets provide great information about subjects, teachers, homework, the cafeteria, maps, and school phone numbers.

high school subjects

not so different after all!

"Learn as much as you can while you are still young,
since life becomes too busy later."

Dana Stewart Scott

One of the changes from going from middle school to high school is the many more subject classes you will attend. You are probably already used to having multiple classes and subjects, but in high school there are tons more to choose from! Funnily enough, you have already been doing these subjects in various forms all throughout your middle school years — you just may not have realized it.

Think about this: during your middle school years, did you ever learn about volcanoes and how they worked? Maybe your science teacher showed you how to construct a model of a volcano out of papier-mâché. There might have been some baking soda involved, plus a little water to simulate lava. Guess what? You were actually having a lesson in geological science!

Or maybe you planted seeds into cotton wool, watered them and watched your seedlings grow over days and then weeks. Guess again — biology! When you wrote poems in class about springtime or wrote a book report — that's all included in the subject of English in high school as well.

What about building replicas of Ancient Egyptian pyramids or sarcophagi? This was part of your foundational education in history and paves the way for you to learn even more about later civilizations, conflicts, and innovations in your History and Social Science classes.

The point of these memories? Simple. You're already prepared for what's coming up in high school years — Science, History, English. Hey, mathematics isn't going to be an alien subject. It'll be just learning new ideas on top of what you've been taught in middle school. You'll be going more in depth with these subjects in high school. And the best news of all — you'll be given help along the way to get you up to speed on the different concepts and skills you'll need.

Sometimes subjects are designed for college preparation. These usually require top grades to attend and are full of future rocket scientists, brain surgeons, and bank presidents. So, with the help of your counselor and parents, you will need to figure out what specific level of class you may be ready to attend.

subjects that may be offered in high school

English

English Literature

Science (e.g., Biology, Chemistry, Physics)

Human Development

Mathematics (e.g., Geometry, Statistics, Calculus)

Physical Education

Food Technology (a fancy title for cooking and studying nutrition)

Health

Home Economics

Sports

History

Geography

Foreign Languages (e.g., French, Spanish, German)

IT (information technology)

Art

Woodwork

Metalwork

Psychology

Music

Drama

Economics

Accounting

Textiles

Visual Communication

Technology

Social Studies

Commerce

Personal Development
Graphics
Technological & Applied
   Science

Visual Arts
Visual Design
and many more…

the new kid on the block

first day nerves!

"Learn from life — learn from the day."

James Rohn

One of my favorite all-time movies stars the actor Owen Wilson, playing the part of a budget bodyguard in *Drillbit Taylor.* It tells the story of a group of boys who are starting their first year of high school. One of the first scenes in the movie shows both friends turning up at the school bus stop dressed the same, wearing identical red shirts.

Picture the shock. There's no time to run home and change, so the pair get on the bus and begin the first day of their high school careers dressed the same. No fun!

Now picture this. It's your first day of high school. You start at your new school and you know absolutely no one, except maybe one guy from church who goes along to your youth group.

Your shoulder's groaning under the weight of a ridiculously heavy school bag. The path to the gate's packed already with kids who actually know their way around.

You reach the first corridor, shuffling on vague memories from an orientation day last month.

Room 7B. Your name's scratched in 8pt on a printout that ran out of ink near your name.

Other 9th graders all around — already best friends, it seems. Groups of chatting 14-year-olds, lots of friendships. Even a few teachers walk by and get in on the conversations.

just me, on my own

The person in the frame is actually a lot like me, back on Day One of high school. I went to a private school in Australia where the kids went all the way from the start of elementary school (called "Prep" in parts of my country) to 12th grade. So, most of the students had known each other since kindergarten. I came from a public school and was the only student making the switch. All my other friends had gone to either the local high or technical school.

So there I was, "new kid on the block," with one friend I hardly knew. Fortunately, I had a lovely first-year teacher that year, Mrs. Gorman, who was very kind and really helped our year's class settle in well from the beginning.

Most kids are especially nervous about that very first day of high school. I know I was! It's perfectly normal to feel nervous and a little unsure about that all-important first day. You might feel somewhat sick or squeamish, and you may even feel like you have a billion butterflies throwing a party in your stomach. Just remember, you're not alone! Many hundreds of thousands of kids all over the world are feeling all the same things as you on their very first day of high school. And they survive — just like *you* will!

tip time
getting the most out of high school!

just remember your first day of high school only happens once, and will go quicker than you can blink.

Many of my students tell me at the end of that very first day that it wasn't nearly as bad as they'd expected. You see, our minds are very powerful things! The brain can expect the future to be horrible, blowing it into something scary and debilitating. The real future, when you actually get there, is often not so bad.

So take this risk — one bold step that might change your life forever. Dare to imagine a brighter first day, a better startup week, an encouraging first year at high school. And tell yourself it'll be okay.

"I'll find my way."

"Someone will help me."

"I'll work out my schedule."

"My bag won't be so heavy tomorrow!"

Many students are actually truly excited about beginning high school. The excitement of a whole new environment, new subjects, responsibilities, and friends is something they are looking forward to and ready to embrace.

No matter what position you're in — whether you are a nervous wreck or insanely excited — just remember your first day of high school only happens once, and will go quicker than you can blink. So get on with it and enjoy your first day!

"I am an old man and have known a great many troubles, but most of them never happened."

Mark Twain

PART 2

A+

getting right on the inside

setting goals

the power of setting goals

"What you get by achieving your goals is not as important
as what you become by achieving your goals."

Zig Ziglar

Imagine this. You head off on a school camping trip for a week in the mountains. It's a hiking camp and you are really excited because you will be hiking with your friends and teacher for three solid days. You arrive at base camp, begin organizing your backpack, then set off with your group for the three-day trek. You begin walking through the glorious forest, and admire the beautiful landscape.

After about five hours, however, you wonder how far you have got to go before you get to your destination for the day to set up for camp.

You call to the teacher, "When will we get to where we're going?"

"I don't know," your teacher replies. "I didn't bring a map. I just thought we'd keep walking until we stopped."

Right about now, you feel nervous. You get slightly anxious about where you are all headed. Right now, you're clearly lost!

And there's probably no cell phone coverage or battery life left in anyone's phones!

Life can be like a long hike. We can walk for what seems like an eternity and not really get anywhere important. That is exactly why setting goals in life is of major importance. We need to have a clear map that we can follow and revise along the way when needed.

Our map is the record of our future goals!

why people don't set goals

80% of life is knowing why
20% of life is knowing how

There are some simple but powerful reasons why people will not set goals:

- They don't understand the importance of setting goals.
- They have never set aside the time.
- They don't know how. (Some people think that just by thinking about getting better grades in English, it will automatically happen!)
- They are afraid of failing or being rejected by their friends or peers.

Setting goals is basically like setting a road map for where you want to go. It helps give you clear directions so you can check in with yourself to make sure you are on track. Put even more simply, a goal is a dream with a date attached to it.

For example, you may decide that when you leave school, you are going to work as a nurse and eventually become a midwife, helping deliver babies.

Just say you are 14 years old now. You probably already have more of an interest in science than your friends. You set yourself goals for the next several years along the following lines:

1. Get good results in science.
2. Study Biology and Anatomy in senior school years.
3. Talk to your career counselor at school about all the possible courses available to you to study nursing.
4. Participate in work experience and volunteer work in a local hospital.
5. Work hard to get the results you need to get into the nursing program that you desire.
6. Begin nursing program.
7. Complete nursing degree.
8. Begin training in midwifery.

A friend of mine, Dale Beaumont, describes goal setting as:

"Deciding on the achievement of a specific objective sometime in the future because of a certain feeling which is obtained as a result of its accomplishment."

Goal setting is one of the most important practices you can learn as a teenager. You will need to be a goal setter if you want to achieve great things with your life. Otherwise, you risk being a drifter!

tip time

getting the most out of high school!

write out your goal and think of it like a dream with a date attached to it.

Your goal right now might be to become better organized, to work on homework for 45 minutes each night, to keep your bedroom tidy, or to be a good friend to others. Whatever your goals are right now, make a commitment to turn them into reality, one step at a time.

You do not have to see the entire journey. Just take the first step in the direction you want to head. In other words, "Take the first bite of the elephant!"

write down your goals

give them flight

"A goal without a plan is just a wish."

Antoine de Saint-Exupery
French Writer (1900-1944)

You give your goals wings when you write them down. That is because you make a commitment to what you want to work at and achieve next.

Maybe your goal is to pass all your end-of-year exams. Your goal sheet might look like this:

1. Find a study partner for English (hardest subject) and Science (second most difficult).
2. Offer to help someone else in Math (my best subject).
3. Ask my English and Science teachers for some practice exams so I can use these in my study time.
4. Set aside Monday and Wednesday evenings for 1 ½ hours to revise content.
5. Pass my exams!

tip time
getting the most out of high school!

put the date next to the goal.
and check it off when it's done.
it's time now for a new goal!

You can do this for any of your goals. The point is, you must write them down and commit to seeing them through. All successful people set clear goals. It is not rocket science. It is simply the way to get things done, to achieve results.

It is also important to note that you should attach a date to each goal that you record. Write the dates in your weekly planner if that helps. Attaching a date to your goals gives you a clear timeline for completing them. Make sure you write out a new one when you have achieved your goal.

set yourself rewards for achieving goals

hey, you deserve something in return!

"You're never a loser until you quit trying."

Mike Ditka

There are times when working toward the goals you have set for yourself is just plain hard work. No one expects you to work and work and not get anything for it. True, you will experience great personal satisfaction from achieving your goals. It is also important, however, to give yourself the occasional reward. Here are just a few of the rewards you could give yourself for achieving goals along the way to your success:

tip time

getting the most out of high school!

large goals are achieved by breaking them up into smaller, bite-sized, achievable pieces.

- Treat yourself to a movie or night out.
- Give yourself one or two nights off from completing work.
- Plan a vacation for when you achieve a major goal.
- Get tickets to see a favorite band close to when you expect to achieve a set goal.
- Plan a fun night in with a group of friends.
- Plan a shopping spree to buy new clothes when you achieve your goal.

If your goal is a fairly big one, don't be put off. Large goals are achieved by breaking them up into smaller, bite-sized, achievable pieces. It can be far too scary to tackle a goal that seems too big from the start. Begin by taking the first small step. Then, once that goal is achieved, take another step. Just keep going. You will get there in the end.

revise your goals often

staying clear of cobwebs

"A goal without a plan is just a wish."

Antoine de Saint-Exupery

It is no use buying a new outfit and leaving it buried in the back of your wardrobe.

Well, as silly as that sounds, such cobweb-attractive behavior is a trap you should avoid. You must check in with yourself often when it comes to setting goals. Do not simply get all enthusiastic, write out your goals and then bury the piece of paper in your bedroom for the next six months.

(If your bedroom is in the same state as most teenagers, you may never even find those goals again until the day you get married and move out!)

Put your goals somewhere clearly visible, daily. Do not write them on a scrap piece of paper but type them up or make them at least look important. You may even like to laminate the page, put a magnet on the back and pop it on the fridge door! Better yet, stick it (sensibly!) to the back of your bathroom door.

tip time

getting the most out of high school!

the bathroom door is a great place to keep yourself mindful of a serious goal!

seek out mentors

wise counsel from experienced people

"Take the first step in faith. You don't have to see
the whole staircase, just take the first step."

Dr. Martin Luther King, Jr. (1929 - 1968)

Mentors are a little like coaches for life. They are people who have usually gone before you and are successful in their chosen fields. In baseball terms, they've got "runs on the board," experience and maturity that you can only benefit from.

The most effective way to be a successful teen and achieve your goals is to seek out such a mentor to help you along the way.

All teenagers need at least one mentor — someone from whom you can seek advice, and who will follow your journey to success.

I was very fortunate, when I was a teenager, to have a couple in my church who were able to mentor me throughout my school years. They kept an eye on me and were the two people I was able to turn to for advice and help if I was experiencing difficulty. That was especially helpful with issues relating to parents.

A mentor could be a teacher from your school, an older student, youth leader, church pastor, uncle, aunt, parent, or grandparent. You may not even know your mentor right now. But the good news is, with the great advancements of computer technology, you can learn from "giants" by reading their advice online.

You can read comments, articles, and speeches by and about people who have been successful in life.

If you want to be a successful basketball player, seek out information about people who are either playing or have had previous success. Many elite athletes have produced an autobiography — a book that discusses their life story — or someone has written about them. Yeah, I know it might seem "Old School," but books can be a terrific resource. They are an amazing source of information and inspiration as to how someone has overcome hurdles and challenges and achieved success in their chosen field. And I would be very surprised if each successful person you followed did not have at least one great mentor from whom he or she also learned.

Write a letter to someone you admire and whose success you would like to achieve. You would probably be surprised that successful people are also normal, everyday people just like you. They have only achieved success because they were driven and set themselves clearly-defined goals. Many successful people get to be that way because they had great mentors in their lives to guide them. They would probably be more than happy to speak to you, or recommend some ideas and directions.

get an attitude!

it can be good for you

"Our attitude is an asset, a treasure of great value which must be protected."

James Rohn

No one else but *you* can control your attitude. Have you ever thought about that?

Just say you get an assignment and you say to yourself right from that moment, "What a stupid assignment. How boring!"

Well, I can bet you right now that you'll probably drag your feet to get that assignment finished, if at all. And it probably won't be your best work at all!

Our experiences are very strongly influenced by our attitude. For example, as a teacher, I have to make a conscious effort each morning before I start the day with my students, that I will have a positive attitude about the day and put a smile on my face. Now, can you just imagine what my days would be like (and the days of my students) if I had a negative attitude about being at school? What would it be like if I just hated spending time each day with my students?

Frankly, the days would drag on, meaningless and boring.

We have all been given a unique and precious gift, and that is the ability to always control our attitude. Sure, bad days will happen and things will go wrong, but we *always have a choice as to what our attitude will be toward these things.*

If you are just about to begin high school, and your attitude had always been pretty poor toward school, do you think things

43

will honestly be any better in high school? Probably not, if you have the same old attitude. I often say to my students when they are just starting high school, "No matter what your attitude was in middle school, and no matter what subjects you struggled with, you can change your attitude right now. And believe me, high school

will be different because you have a choice to totally change your attitude."

Be positive about the new experiences. Your past experiences don't define what your new experiences will be. You need to have an attitude — and it should be a good one!

One of the problems is the word itself — "ATTITUDE." The way we use it nowadays ("She's got an attitude" or "He's got an attitude problem") is always clouded in negativity.

The truth is, a good attitude is just as powerful if you're willing to have one.

An "attitude" is simply a state of mind — how you think and act. So why not decide to have a positive, "*I can do it*" attitude! You see, it's not the circumstances and problems that we encounter that matter (and you'll encounter many, that's for certain). It's your attitude and how you respond that really matters.

I really admire the example set by a guy named Justin Herald. I have shared this story in a previous book, but I loved it so much I've decided to highlight it again here.

He was just an ordinary young man who, by his own account, didn't do too well in school. Some of his teachers complained to him that he had an attitude problem. One teacher in particular,

Justin recalls, told him that he wouldn't get anywhere in life (or words to that effect) and that he would probably end up dead or living on the streets.

Well, as the story goes (and it's a true story), Justin Herald *did* have an attitude problem. As a young guy, with only $50 in his bank account, he decided to use his attitude problem for the better, and came up with some attitude slogans. Phrases such as "If I want your opinion I'll ask for it!"

With his small amount of cash, he organized the purchase of some T-shirts and screen printed his attitude slogans on the front of them. Before long, Attitude Inc. was formed. People purchased his new attitude T-shirts by the truckload. Before Justin knew it, he had used his attitude to begin a multi-million dollar business that is still thriving today!

Recently, Justin told the story of how he was at one of the clothing stores near where he lived, that stocked his T-shirts. In front of the store, he bumped into his previous teacher who had openly "dissed" him in high school.

The teacher said: "Ah, Justin Herald. I'm surprised to see you still alive! I knew you wouldn't get anywhere in life."

Justin just bit his lip and smiled. Because that teacher was actually wearing one of Justin's shirts — and he had *no idea* that Justin's successful company produced them!

You see, it's all about your attitude!

Don't ever let anyone tell you that you can't achieve something, or that you are hopeless. You are not! People who have to always give an opinion about you or want to cut you down when you share your hopes and dreams, are just being negative and have no business trying to shove their bad attitude on you.

Instead, do what Justin did and take that attitude to drive you to succeed in whatever you choose to do with your life.

it's okay to make mistakes

avoid the regrets ahead of time

"Fall seven times, stand up eight."

Japanese Proverb

Throughout your high school years (and beyond!) you *will* make mistakes — that's a given. In fact, we can't grow if we ***don't*** make mistakes. The important thing is that we *learn* from the mistakes we make. You'd be crazy to keep on making the same mistakes and expect to get better wouldn't you?

Take Math, for example. Let's say you've just received your test back from your teacher. You realize that you didn't pass the test. It's not surprising, as you didn't actually study for it! Your teacher tells you that you are more than capable of passing this test as you know how to solve the problems — you just hadn't practiced!

So you've already got a plan for next time. Study. Practice. And be prepared ahead of the test rather than worrying about it as you walk into the classroom to actually take the exam.

It's not always a bad thing to fail or make mistakes. The main thing is that you learn your lesson from the failure.

> ## tip time
> getting the most out of high school!
>
> *one mistake isn't a failure. neither is a 2nd, 3rd, and so on...*
> *but failing to learn from the setbacks is a mistake you'll only re-live and regret.*

Thomas Edison made many hundreds of mistakes, or failures, before he finally invented a functioning filament in the form of a working light globe. Rather than just giving up after the 100th or even 300th try, he remained determined. He knew that eventually he would find success... and he did!

friends and peers!

making an investment

"The most important trip you may take is meeting people halfway."

Henry Boye

As I write this chapter, I have just returned from a beautiful wedding of a friend I went to high school with more than 20 years ago. Can you believe it? She wanted to have some of her old school friends at her wedding as it was important for her to have people she has known since she was a teenager. It was really special to catch up with some of the girls and guys I knew when I was 13, then just a gangly teenager!

I also have a couple of very dear friends that I have known since my later high school years. They befriended me when I made the very difficult transition to a very strict private school, with many rules and regulations to abide by. They guided and supported me through some pretty difficult times during high school, especially settling in and learning the ropes. We have since gone on to support each other through our various career choices, marriages and babies. Now, more than 20 years later, we still make a regular time to catch up and will remain lifelong friends. That's one of the awesome results from sticking it out through high school. (Thanks Annie and Vanessa!)

When I speak to young people about the reasons why they do or don't enjoy their high school experience, one of the most common automatic responses has to do with friendships and social interactions. In fact, friends and peer groups are one of the highest priorities in the lives of most teenagers, so it makes sense that the bulk of this time interacting occurs in school.

Friendships built throughout your high school years can indeed be a lifelong and wonderful bond.

At times, some kids really struggle at making friends. School days can be tough and isolating. Lonely at times. If that's you, and you really hate school due to friendship issues, be assured — you are NOT ALONE! There are many young people out there who struggle socially at school. I know that may not seem very reassuring right now, but there are some useful tips we'll look at in this book that may help you expand your social network at school.

I remember a girl I knew in high school. She cried to me about not having friends, not having anyone to notice that she was so alone. She'd even sat in a toilet stall during one whole lunchtime and felt she hadn't been noticed missing.

There are many young people out there who struggle socially at school.

Stepping back from the emotion she felt, the physical isolation she caused by locking herself in the stall was actually the problem. The truth is, she *had* been missed. People didn't know where she had gone and assumed she might have been spending time with others.

She really needed to get out and give other people a chance to get to know her.

You, too, are worth getting to know and you have a great deal to offer other people — namely, your friendship. But you will often (not always) need to take the first step and give others an opportunity to get to know you!

Ralph Waldo Emerson was so right when he said, "The only way to have a friend is to be one first." When you really stop and think about it, can you really expect to have great friends if you aren't willing to step out and be one first?

Perhaps you're really shy, and that's okay. Some people are not very outgoing, and I'm not asking you to change your personality. But you will need to sometimes step out of your *comfort* zone and into your *courage* zone and take that first step to say hello to someone. I assure you that you'll be surprised once you start making conversation with others.

Have you ever sat at home and thought to yourself, "Why hasn't anyone called me?" Good question... until you think to yourself, "Hey, when was the last time I called someone?"

It takes two to make a great friendship work. And you will get out of a friendship exactly what you put into it.

A+

"To the world you may just be one person,
but to one person you may be the world."

Brandy Snyder

"Choose a smile, not a frown."

James Rohn

"True friends will be there with you to share the giggles
in the good times
And cry with you in the bad times."

Anonymous

"Fate chooses your relations. You choose your friends."

Jacques Delille

"The antidote for 50 enemies is one friend."

Aristotle

"I have learned that to have a good friend is the purest of all God's
gifts, for it is love that has no exchange or payment."

Frances Farmer

"It is one of the blessings of old friends
that you can afford to be stupid with them."

Ralph Waldo Emerson

THOUGHTS ON...FRIENDSHIP

"The proper office of a friend is to side with you when you are wrong. Nearly everyone will side with you when you are in the right."

Mark Twain

"Never refuse any advance of friendship, for if nine out of ten bring you nothing, one alone may repay you."

Madame de Tencin

"Friendship consists of forgetting what one gives, and remembering what one receives."

Alexandre Dumas

"Friendship is the hardest thing in the world to explain. It's not something you learn in school. But if you haven't learned the meaning of friendship, you haven't learned anything."

Muhammad Ali

"A friend is a gift you give yourself."

Robert Louis Stevenson

"Friendship and support from friends is something which is a source of tremendous inspiration always and to everyone."

Nelson Mandela

"You can make more friends in two months by becoming really interested in other people, than you can in two years by trying to get other people interested in you."

Dale Carnegie

important qualities to look for in friends

❏ **Honesty** – good friends will always tell you the truth, even if they know it's not what you want to hear.

❏ **Acceptance** – true friends will accept you for the wonderful person that you are – they will love you for the good parts and the not-so-good parts, because of who you are.

❏ **Relatability** – Friends share your passions and interests, but also understand that they don't have to love everything you like.

❏ **Listeners** – friends will be there just to listen, if that's what you need. Sometimes just sharing a problem or exciting news can make all the difference.

❏ **Stickability** – good friends will always stick right by you, especially if you're being bullied or have made a mistake (as we all do from time to time).

when a friendship is unhealthy

no room for two on one-way streets

"True happiness consists not in the multitude
of friends but in the worth and choice."

Ben Johnson

Unhealthy friendships can feel kind of like a vacuum cleaner sucking all the energy out of you. It's all heading one way!

In other words, unhealthy friendships are one sided – that is, one person is always doing the work and having to help out the other one. While it is true that all great friendships will be tested at times, and each will go through difficulties at certain points in your lives, it is important to remember that it is just like a partnership. And it needs to work for both of you!

Needy friends can be quite difficult – the friend who has a low self image and is always complaining about being "too fat" or "too ugly"... There is only a certain amount of this that people can take. My advice here is simple... be a good friend yourself! Affirm your friends, reminding them that they are important and worthwhile people.

On the issue of body shape and size, it's a good idea to not get caught in that mental

tip time

getting the most out of high school!

if you're worried about a friend, tell someone.

battle. Of course, if you are worried about a friend's health, make sure you tell a trusted adult. Otherwise, try to ignore negative behavior as it will only seek to bring *you* down, and **you** don't need that!

If you have a friend or peer who is into things that you know are just wrong and not okay... *RUN A MILE!!!* If such a person is a close friend, of course this can be difficult, because you don't want to abandon a person making unhealthy choices. But you do not want to nurture a friendship with someone whom you know is making a deliberate choice to do things that are dangerous or unhealthy.

I have been really fortunate in my life that I have always been drawn to fantastic girls as my friends. I have always made friends with people who have similar qualities and attitudes as me. That really helps. You will find that most people you develop friendships with will share similar beliefs and interests.

peer pressure

to sand or not to sand

Think back to your first days in a preschool or just starting out in kindergarten. Someone says, "Throw that sand on Johnny!" You look down and see you're in a sandbox. Just near your undone shoe laces are two things.

First, there's a lot of sand!

Second, you notice the undone shoelaces of a fellow sandbox explorer. Must be Johnny! The guy who's become the focus of attention from a bully nearby.

The bully wants you to help him out, to hassle the other kid in the sandbox. The bully wants a new recruit: you.

"Yeah, go ahead!" Master Bully repeats to you. "Throw sand on that kid next to you. In his face! C'mon!"

What do you do?

Peer pressure started then. Even in a sandbox. Pressure to do someone's bidding. To throw sand on someone else. To let yourself be a slave to another's plans and desires.

> ### tip time
> getting the most out of high school!
>
> *throwing sand at someone can be pretty silly... especially when the wind picks up!*

Interesting, isn't it? Early years. Not just high school. You see, peer pressure doesn't just magically appear on day one of 9th Grade, despite the bad reputation the high school years can have.

56

Back there in the sandbox, you made the right choice (hopefully!) to hold off on the sand throwing. To make your own decision.

So too, in high school, you'll be better off resisting the temptation to follow the pressure of another, or a group of others.

As you went through middle school, the choices you faced might have been a little more advanced, like whether to follow friends and sneak off campus during break periods, for example.

You always have a choice to make when it comes to peer pressure. In high school, the pressure might just be another step up — "Do I make a decision not to attend a science class?" "Do I ditch with a group of buddies and miss a day of school?" "Do I leave the school grounds and have a cigarette?"

Don't be fooled into thinking that entry to high school equals a massive weight of pressure to do things you don't want to do. You always have a choice as to the decisions you will make.

It's a great idea to make these types of decisions *before* you are faced with them. You can do that by deciding what type of person you want to be. Do you want to be a person who is often known as a "sheep" and just does what people tell him or her to do?

Sheep don't want to look silly in front of the flock for making a stand. So they just go along with the flock. Don't be like that. Decide now that you'll always choose the best decision for you, no matter what. That way, it won't be so difficult when you are faced with the pressure to do something you're not comfortable with.

choose your influences

have a look at who's nearby

If you hang around negative people all the time, chances are pretty high that you will soon become a fairly negative person. In fact, other people's attitudes and opinions can have a huge impact on us.

Have you ever been put in a group to work on a class assignment? You find that the teacher has put you with two highly unmotivated people, aka[1] "lazy!" Often, the motivated student is dragged down by the rest of the group's negativity and lack of focus. Then notice the difference in the group's productivity as soon as you put two motivated students with a fairly negative and unmotivated person. The positive students will quite often motivate the team to achieve its collective best and complete an amazing assignment.

The people we choose to spend our time with have a great influence – both positive and negative – on us.

What sort of people do you choose to hang out with?

For example, a teen girl began hanging with a negative crowd. They were part of a local gang whose members spent a lot of time at the local 7-Eleven, harassing others, smoking, and using foul language.

Most of the 7-Eleven teens lived in government-funded housing for troubled youth. The way they saw it, they were free from rules and restrictions, all the time. That's what they told the teen girl whom they welcomed into their group.

---

1 'aka' – if you're not already familiar with the term, it just means 'also known as'.

She believed them. Their life looked pretty sweet. Back at home, her parents had rules and restrictions — the way she saw it, the rules were holding her back.

The girl soon began allowing negative influences to change her attitude throughout her life, affecting the way she spoke to parents and teachers.

If you hang around with the wrong people for too long, you soon will become just like the people your parents warn you against. If you choose to spend your time with a person who does not care about school or achieving good grades, soon you will not care much either.

Make a choice, instead, to spend your time with people who have a positive influence on your life and your self-image. Spend time with friends who build you up rather than tear you and others down.

A+

Q&A time...

Q: I really enjoy reading at lunchtime as it gives me a break from everything, and I can't seem to put my book down. But I'm new in high school and really want to make friends with new people. What should I do?

That's a really great question, and one that is actually quite a common problem among many students (those who love reading anyway).

Choose one or two lunchtimes per week in which you can read or hang out in the library. Keep the other three free for socializing and making new friends. It's okay to read, and I'd encourage that. However, making friends and interacting with other students is just as important because you are building up a social and support network.

The same can be said if you love drawing or any other activity that can be done in isolation. It's important to have interests that you can do by yourself, but make sure you allow plenty of time to be social.

Q: I have a really great friend at school and we enjoy hanging out together. But sometimes she goes off with other friends at lunch and leaves me out completely. How should I handle this? It's making life at school awful!

Social life at school and friendship issues can cause a lot of heartache at different times during high school. In fact, it would be pretty rare if you didn't experience being left out of a social group at some point. So what I'm saying first of all is, you're not alone here!

Sometimes, our friends want to expand their social network a bit as well. That's not to say that they like us any less, but it certainly can feel pretty horrible and isolating at the same time.

My suggestion would be to try to branch out on your own a little too. Look for other students who might seem like outsiders or don't seem to have many social groups. You could certainly use this as an opportunity to make some other new friends; not to replace your friends, but just broaden your social network. You might be surprised by the new friends you'll make along the way.

ask sharon

got a question for the author? drop sharon a line by email:

sharon@sharonwitt.com.au

gossip

sticks and stones...
really *do* hurt as much as words

"Whoever gossips **to** you
will gossip **about** you."

Spanish proverb

By far, hurtful gossiping and cattiness can be one of the most difficult parts of being an adolescent girl.

A definition I use for "gossip" could be anything said that you wouldn't be perfectly happy to say in front of the person involved.

But, more importantly, the effect is longer-lasting than the time it takes for the comment to be made.

Gossip can be one of the most soul-destroying things a person can experience. It can be like lighting a match in the middle of a forest. At first, only a few small twigs are lit and a small flame grows, then that flame catches onto another branch and before you know it, the whole forest is on fire.

Do you remember the game in which a group of children sit in a circle and an original message is passed from one person to the next? The first sentence is changed as it works its way through the group, quietly being passed from one person to the next. As each message is passed along, bits and pieces of the original words get left out or changed. By the time the message returns around the circle it may not sound anything like the intended sentence.

Gossiping is a lot like that game. As people pass on information about another person, they can often add their own slant on the story or exaggerate parts that sound better. By the time the hurtful gossip gets around, it can be very far removed from the actual truth and that's where extreme damage can be done to the subject of the gossip.

I have a really simple guidepost for deciding if something is gossip or not: Ask yourself the following question before continuing to pass on information:

"Will this information build the other person up (make them feel great about themselves), or damage someone's self image? Will I make that person feel bad?"

It's pretty simple, really. You will know, in your "heart," whether the information is helpful or not. Use your intuition!

"Watch the way you talk. Let nothing foul or dirty come out of your mouth. Say only what helps, each word a gift."

Ephesians 4:29 (The Message)

"Don't be bluffed into silence by the threats of bullies. There's nothing they can do to your soul, your core being."

Matthew 10:28a (The Message)

"The only time people dislike gossip is when you gossip about them."

Will Rogers

"Words kill, words give life; they're either poison or fruit — you choose."

Proverbs 18:21 (The Message)

"Gossiping is something wrong, something bad.
If you spread secrets, the person who it's about
Will have a permanent scar
They will never be able to totally forget about it.
This person can't talk to her friends any more
Because they have hurt her too many times.
Are you one of the friends?
Do you treat your friends this way?
Well if you are, you need to know,
It's not the right way to treat your friends.
Soon it won't be a problem though,
Because you won't have any friends left."

Taylor Dykstra

parents — getting along

asher's outside... oops!

"Intelligent children listen to their parents;
foolish children do their own thing."

Proverbs 13:1 (The Message)

Christmas has just passed as I'm writing this. And our family's just grown by one.

No, I haven't had another child, although it sometimes feels that way! The newcomer has fur and four legs — a cat, well, a kitten, to be precise! "Asher," the adorable kitten.

Now, we love this little kitten so much and want to give him loads of cuddles. We make sure we know where he is all the time. He's just still so tiny!

At the moment, he stays inside with us, but every now and then, we take Asher out into the backyard for a little exploring time. He stays close though.

Now, in about six months time, little Asher will be fully grown and will reach full maturity. By then, we'll be letting him go out more, enjoying more freedom.

We won't always be right next to him. So, Asher might make some mistakes of judgement. He may even get into some fights with the neighbors' two cats. I expect the occasional scratched nose as he explores those boundaries! But, hopefully, he'll remember where he lives and come back home.

A pet who matures and doesn't need you around so much is a little like your relationship with your parents. They love you more than anything, and don't want anything to happen to you. They don't want you to make mistakes, but they know you will and will still be there for you when you do.

Many young people find that their relationship often goes through a gradual change once they enter high school. It's not that all of a sudden you become totally mature. It's more of a gradual process. But it's certainly true that once you begin high school, there's an emphasis placed on you developing greater responsibility for your own learning — and in many other areas probably.

Now it's also quite normal for you to feel during these high school years that your parents just don't *get* you! That's pretty common. And it's not that they don't get you, but your parents are trying to grow and change *with* you. All these growing pains can be pretty daunting for them too.

There isn't some big, grand rule book that comes with teenagers. True, you do need to take on greater responsibilities and you'll want to be able to do more than you were allowed to do when you were in middle school, but you have to learn to do it gradually. Let your parents see how responsible you can be in the small things first; then you can build up to bigger things.

tip time
getting the most out of high school!

remember parents are people too! really!

Like any relationship, communication and honesty is important. You need to show your parents care and respect if that is what you seek in return. Despite what you might think, parents have feelings too and are mostly just trying to do their best in parenting you — sometimes they might seem too strict or in a bad mood, but just remember that you feel like that too sometimes.

Think about how you treat your friends for a moment. Are you generally kind, honest and respectful every time you talk? Most of the time, you are. You should also treat your parents in the same way — this makes for a healthy and respectful relationship. Even when you're having emotional or "blahhh" days, try your best not to take it out on the people who love you the most and matter most to you — because they love you more than anyone!

"Children, do what your parents tell you. This is only right. 'Honor your father and mother' is the first commandment that has a promise attached to it, namely, 'so you will live well and have a long life.'"

Ephesians 6:1-3 (The Message)

hints for getting along with parents

❏ Be honest! Talking honestly with your parents is the best way to keep your relationship sweet.

❏ Share your life with them! That doesn't mean you have to tell them your every thought or everything that happens, but share stuff with them occasionally to stay connected.

❏ Keep to your word! When you tell your parents that you'll be home at a certain time, stick to it. This will ensure that you build trust and your parents won't worry themselves sick.

❏ Ask for help! Even though you might feel that your parents don't know a thing, why not occasionally ask for their help? Most likely, your parents will really like it if you ask for advice. No matter what, your parents love you and you can always call on them when you need them — no matter what time it is!

❏ Speak up! Try to talk with your parents as often as you can.

tip time
getting the most out of high school!

ask your parents for advice. they'll appreciate the trust you show in their opinions.

❏ Hug your parents! Nothing mends a tense situation or heals a relationship better than a good, old-fashioned hug.

taking care of your health

staying healthy

"No day is so bad it can't be fixed with a nap."

Carrie Snow

It's important to keep yourself clean and healthy, especially during your high school years so you can grow into a healthy young adult. Some of you have already entered puberty, and have begun to notice an increase in your sweat — particularly your underarms. For girls, as you begin menstruation, it is even more important to shower daily.

Don't neglect your teeth either! They are an important part of our health and need to be brushed and flossed daily to remove plaque and to prevent bad breath and gum disease.

tip time
getting the most out of high school!

you'll benefit from using deodorant... your friends will appreciate the effort too!

If you find that you sweat a lot, use a good anti-perspirant deodorant under your arms. Remember also to clean your face daily to remove grime and dirt that builds up in your pores.

get a good night's sleep!

The average teenager needs about ten hours of sleep a night, but many get as little as six hours or less! You actually do most of your growing while you are sleeping, so it's important that you rest well. Try to avoid staying up to all hours listening to music on your iPhone or watching television. Instead, read a good book (like this one!) in bed to calm yourself and set your body up for a good night's sleep. Avoid drinks with caffeine in them such as coffee and soda. Have a hot chocolate instead. Remember, your mood will be much better the next day if you have had enough sleep.

Trying to last through the rigors of daily school life is a lot more difficult when you are not feeling energized! So do yourself a favor and give yourself permission to have plenty of sleep.

Tips for Staying Healthy!

- ❏ Shower daily
- ❏ Use a good antiperspirant deodorant
- ❏ Wash your face daily
- ❏ Get lots of sleep (aim for 8-10 hours)
- ❏ Drink plenty of water (8 glasses per day is what you should aim for!)
- ❏ Brush and floss your teeth twice daily!

take care of *you*!

the dirty car's groaning under grime!

Imagine you have finally purchased your dream car. Shiny at first. A thing of beauty.

You drive it around with pride and visit all your friends. You cannot, however, be bothered washing it, so a mountain of dirt and grease builds up over the first year.

You drive and drive the car, but you forget to check the oil and water, not to mention filling the tank with gas.

How far do you think you would get? I can tell you now that it would not be long before your prized car would break down. It cannot continue to run without constant attention and good fuel.

Our bodies are kind of like cars. They need constant fuel and care in order to keep them running at their optimum.

I read once how we should look after our bodies because they are the only houses we have. We only get one body, so we really need to take the time to care for it.

tip time
getting the most out of high school!

eight glasses of water a day. enough said!

diet

Be mindful of your diet. In these days of junk and processed foods, make sure you try to get at least three servings of fruit and vegetables per day. Likewise, our bodies are made up of more

71

than 50 percent water. This means that we need to ensure we replace our fluids constantly. Two liters (eight glasses) of water per day is recommended.

Try filling a 1.5 liter plastic bottle with water at the beginning of the day. Carry this bottle around with you and drink from it wherever you go. If this sounds like too much, fill a smaller bottle regularly throughout the day. If water is too boring for you, cut a small slice of lemon or lime and pop it in your bottle.

exercise

away from the computer screen

Keep your body healthy by making sure you exercise it regularly. In an age when video games and DVDs are all the rage, ensure you get out and actually *MOVE!* Walk places as often as you can and try to get involved in a regular sport. (No! A video game is not a sport!) Get active to keep blood pumping around your body.

- Walk the dog, or somebody else's.
- Go for a run.
- Go for a hike with friends.
- Take an aerobics class.
- Take up a sport (e.g., volleyball, baseball, soccer).
- Join the local gym.
- Try rowing or canoeing.
- Callisthenics.
- Dancing.
- Gymnastics.
- Boxing.
- Wrestling.

tip time
getting the most out of high school!

being overly vigorous with a wireless controller doesn't really qualify as an active, regular sport!

stress

signs worth noting

There is no doubt that entering high school can be a very stressful time. You are coping with huge changes including:

- High school/homework pressures
- New school environment
- New teachers
- Physical changes (puberty)
- Emotions
- Parents
- Friendships

It is really important that you find healthy outlets for dealing with any stress that you feel. Some people deal with stress by exercising or talking with friends. Make sure you find the outlet that best suits *you*, and make sure you take action.

One of the biggest stress indicators is illness, so make sure you take stress seriously and take care of yourself.

stress signs:

- Inability to sleep properly.
- Not being able to eat — disinterest in food.
- Lack of interest in friends and things that you usually enjoy doing.
- Crying often or feeling down in the dumps.
- A feeling of being unable to cope.

If you are struggling with any of the above symptoms for a few weeks, you could be struggling with stress. It is important that you talk with your parents, teacher, or school counselor. It would also be good for your parents or guardians to arrange for you to visit your local doctor to get a thorough examination.

tip time
getting the most out of high school!

stress relief comes in different ways; what works for someone else doesn't necessarily have to be the rule you follow.

stress busters

if you are feeling a bit stressed,
try some of the following solutions...

- **Exercise.** This is great for relieving stress, because your body will release its own natural, "feel good" chemicals. It also helps the blood flow better throughout your body, giving it a great boost.
- **Go for a long walk.** Take a stroll around your neighborhood or local park. Getting some fresh air on a quiet walk can help clear your head.
- **Have a couple of early nights.** If you are stressed, this could be a sign that your body needs some rest. Make yourself a warm drink (like hot chocolate or a caffeine-free tea), grab a good book, and read for a little while before having a good, long sleep. You need between eight and ten hours of sleep per night to feel well rested and stress-free. Make sleep a priority, and your other priorities will fall into place.
- **Eat well.** Fill your body with lots of fruit and vegetables. This may sound kind of boring, but spending a few days giving your body extra minerals and vitamins will help restore you.
- **Rent your favorite comedy movie** from the DVD store or rent it online! Laughter also releases your body's natural endorphins that help make you feel better.

- **Do something you love doing** — Paint, draw, write, hike, ride, or make something. What is your passion?
- **Spend a day out with friends** — Go shopping, skateboard, ride your bike, go hiking; just hang out together.

dealing with bullying

before, during, and after high school

Bullying is, unfortunately, something that many kids associate with high school. And that's a big shame because many kids make it through high school without any experience of bullying whatsoever.

But if it does happen, it can occur in elementary school just as easily as high school, and even in the workforce.

I guess bullying is often associated with high school because it can seem more prevalent, since there are usually many more students and more social groups that can lead to more problems.

When most of us think of bullying, it's easy to think of someone being backed into a corner of a classroom when the teacher is out of the room – an image of someone being verbally threatened or actually physically assaulted.

I remember, as a 7th grade student, new to my school, being locked in the storeroom cupboard of the classroom by a tall student. That was just because I was the new girl and she didn't really like me.

But, in fact, while physical bullying does still unfortunately occur, it is the emotional type of bullying that can be just as hurtful and can leave lasting memories and effects.

examples of bullying

- Physically hitting, punching, or shoving another person, intentionally.
- Name calling.

- Deliberately provoking someone, making fun of them.
- Encouraging someone to do something he or she does not want to do.
- Excluding someone from a group's activities.
- Gossiping.
- Writing hurtful or nasty emails, Facebook posts, letters, IMs, or text messages.

a bullying example

real life beyond the tv screen

"Treat everyone the same, by treating them different.
Respect people's differences."

Author unknown

I saw a woman on a talk show — then in her late 30s — complaining how she could not move forward in her life. She explained how she had suffered immense emotional and verbal bullying 20 years prior.

The culprit had been a fellow female student at her high school. The victim had become pregnant as a teenager and suffered a great deal of verbal abuse from other girls and one "popular and attractive" girl in particular. Both women were reunited on the show in front of a studio audience.

The victim was still, to that day, absolutely devastated by the childhood bullying.

She had carried around a burden of rejection and hurt for two decades.

The most frightening thing was the reaction of the alleged bully. She claimed she had no recollection of the girl on stage or of the verbal attacks she had made.

She apologized but remained incredulous at the degree of hurt.

sticks and stones

what a load of garbage!

Name-calling is bullying. Think about this famous expression: "Sticks and stones may break my bones but words will never hurt me." What a load of garbage!

I can vividly recall verbal bullying, way back as a 12 year-old, in 7th grade. I have always been someone of small stature, and was easily the smallest in my class back then.

One fellow student came up with the nickname "weasel" for me. I absolutely hated that. It made me feel like some awful little animal. Why couldn't they think up a title like "little cutie" or something like that?

Well, I coped pretty well, until the last day of the school year when our class teacher was giving out Christmas cards (my school year began in January and ended in December). They were lovely, hand-made cards with caricatures of ourselves on the front. As mine came around, I couldn't believe my eyes; right there above my very cute portrait was the word "Weasel!" I couldn't believe that even my teacher had picked up on that name!

Well, I am still small in stature, but I don't let it bother me.

I tell this story to illustrate, though, that names stick! Some 25 years later, I can still recall that experience as though it was yesterday.

tip time
getting the most out of high school!

call me "little cutie" next time you meet me. I won't answer to the other title!

your tongue—a sword?

ignoring is easier said than done

You may be a person who occasionally calls people names, for whatever reason. You need to understand that the words that come out of your mouth can have a lasting effect on someone, though you may not think so at the time.

You may say, "Oh, but they know that I'm only joking." Well they may *say* that, but words have a way of sticking in our minds, if they are offensive or hurtful. And people will, when they're alone, replay those words over and over again. (If you're the victim, be encouraged to turn the replay button off in your mind to those words!)

So please, remember that your tongue is a very powerful weapon, and even though you may not physically hurt someone, you can cause real emotional damage.

You need to make sure that the words that come out of your mouth will not cause someone else to feel bad. Use your words to build others up, not destroy a person's self image.

people keep bullying me!

So what should you do if you are currently a victim of bullying?

The usual advice is to "just ignore" the bully.

But that is easier said than done. The most important thing for you to remember is that you are unique and valued! Your value is not in what others think of you or say about you. The most important thing is that you believe that you are amazing and valuable. You also need to know that the people who bully others usually do so for a reason. They may have a lot of their own difficult issues of self-worth. The main reason why people bully others is that they see elements of value in others that they wish they had. So they try to wear their victim down.

It's about jealousy, really. And control.

Also, remember that people can only put you down as far as you will allow them to. Here's the trick then: don't merely ignore. If you choose to ignore them **and** choose to listen to the positive words people speak to you, then you retain control over your life.

tip time

getting the most out of high school!

bullies are the ones with the real problems in life — not you!

So try it! Next time someone says something negative to you, repeat a positive affirmation (positive word or phrase) to yourself inside your head. You could say something to yourself like, "I know that I am worthwhile and important," or "I am beautiful and lovely." You should feel much better. And of course, if the bullying becomes abusive or physical, tell an adult!

It is also important to remember that if you cannot say something positive to someone, don't say anything at all.

bully busters

ignore your bully

Bullies actually get their power from you, only if you give it away. Every time you react, you give the bully the result they were after. Ignoring someone takes away all their bully power and it all comes back to you!

say NO

As soon as you say this single, powerful word, you are letting bullies know loud and clear that what they are doing or saying is not okay. If you struggle a little with this at first, start by saying it under your breath or in your mind until you soon have the courage to say it out loud and with authority. You are worth it! Saying "No" loud and clear also lets everyone else around you know that what is happening is not okay. They are a witness to what is happening and your desire for it not to happen again!

> ### tip time
> getting the most out of high school!
>
> *bullies are actually people with no confidence in life... they just want to rob yours!*

get help

If you are at school, it is really important that you let a teacher or counselor know as soon as you are the victim of a bully. Most schools have in place (or should have) very strict anti-bullying

policies. If you cannot talk to your teacher, ask a friend to go on your behalf or go with you.

Talk to your parents. They will deal with this on your behalf, and can talk to your teacher or school principal.

stand tall and have confidence

Bullies are looking for someone from whom they can steal confidence. Try to remember that a bully is really just someone who is lacking confidence in his or herself. A bully tries to make others feel inferior to hide insecurities. When you remember this, you realize the bully is just a person who lacks confidence.

don't look the other way
if you see someone being bullied

If you see a friend or someone else being bullied, you owe it to them to let someone know, or to step in for them. Make sure you do not get involved with a situation of physical bullying; rather, call for assistance. Looking the other way and ignoring a bullying situation is just as bad as being the bully yourself.

PART 3

A+

getting the most out of high school

let's get organized

answering chaos with order

Imagine walking into a doctor's surgery and having to step over a pile of papers, books, trash, and clothes just to reach the examination chair. I'm guessing you would get the impression that the doctor was not too serious about being a doctor.

It might be a giveaway that he's hurrying you along when he does see you, or maybe it's the fact he's more focused on golf-putting practice in the surgery waiting room rather than answering the intercom.

In life, we need to have some sort of system to get organized, otherwise we tend to feel a little out of control and not sure what we should do next.

Just like with the golf-crazy doctor, you'd be able to tell a lot by looking at a teenager's bedroom. If it's chaos city, that says something about their state of mind. Chances are the teen is probably feeling that things are hectic and confused with life in general.

Get yourself a cool planner. This is one of the best tools to help you get organized, especially for school or work.

Here's the thing... TODAY, you can begin to organize your life better. You can start by organizing your bedroom at home. Set aside an afternoon (or a whole week, if it's that bad!) to find a home for all your possessions. You can buy inexpensive boxes or plastic containers from a local discount shop, or even cover some old shoe boxes in fun paper. Then start labeling!

Make sure you label your boxes clearly so you know where to find things when you need them.

Things you can organize into boxes:

- Photographs
- School projects
- Makeup
- CDs, DVDs, and video games
- Letters and cards from friends and family
- Keepsakes, journals, special cards

You'll feel so much better once you begin to organize yourself.

It's true that some people do not find this easy. It doesn't seem to come naturally. And that's okay. If I'm talking to you, then I'm sure you have skills in other areas that are going to be just as special as someone who cannot wait to get up each morning to file notes! But it's no excuse for chaos.

It might seem like a big job. Sure. But you could always ask for help, especially from another family member or friend who's better at organizing than you are.

Start simple. Get yourself a cool planner. This is one of the best tools to help you get organized, especially for school or work.

For school, you can use different colored markers to label different homework subjects and assignments. As you go, you can check off work when it has been completed.

being organized for high school

help is at hand for the tornado victims

Oh yes! My favorite part of entering high school! This subject causes many a student to crumble into a quivering mess on the floor at the mere mention of it. Ok, well maybe not a quivering mess, but it certainly causes many adolescents stress and worry, especially those who are totally disorganized!

As humans, we are not naturally born as super organized beings. It is very much a learned trait or habit. The great news is that there is a great deal of help out there to help you get organized and on top of everything — whether you are about to begin high school or you are halfway through and trying to sort yourself out!

Those students who usually survive quite well with the schoolwork side of high school are mostly those who have developed good, solid, organizational habits.

Don't worry if this doesn't describe you! If your bedroom and schoolbag resemble the after-effects of a tornado, don't worry. Help is at hand!!

Free Gift

For some cool organization labels for your folders and homework station, go to **www.survivinghighschool.com.au** and download your free labels. They're ready to print from your home computer and use to get organized.

the basics — what you need for high school

why did you bring a tractor to class?
I said, "protractor!"

Before starting high school, you'll most likely be given a supply list and book list by the school that will contain all the books and tools that you'll need for each of your subjects.

It might seem like just another list of "must haves" that you really couldn't care less about. Or maybe something that would just interest your parents in the last week of summer!

But these lists are actually an incredible resource guide for getting you organized at school. They'll contain the items you will need to do two things... One, to keep your teacher happy ("I'm impressed

tip time
getting the most out of high school!

a pen is mightier than a music player if you want to impress your English teacher!

you've got your spare loose leaf refill sheets, Sharon!"). Two, they'll make your life easier and might even impress your parents ("Sharon, as your mother, I am so impressed you knew where to find that spare binder we bought you!")

You'd be surprised how many students I've come across in my teaching career who arrive to class without the basic and essential materials. For example, they might turn up to an English class without their pencil cases, pens or even so much as books to write in. Can you imagine? How on earth can you expect to get anything of significance out of a lesson, without so much as bothering to even bring something to write with! (Okay, that's the bit where I rant a little as a teacher, but please forgive me; it only happens during the beginning of the school year... then, I'm all good!)

Seriously though, these students I'm talking about — not you, of course! — will often waste ten or so minutes disrupting other students, and the teacher, trying to borrow a pen and something to write on.

While we're on the topic of coming prepared to class, try to avoid bringing things that will distract you from getting the most out of your lesson and completing your work. Can you guess the items I am imagining? iPods, cell phones (probably banned from school anyway), non-school journals, toys, gadgets, hairbrush, lip gloss, toy cars, and tractors. (YES! I've seen them all!)

the basics!

Ruler

Pens in red, blue, black and
    even green, if you like

Colored pencils

Grey lead pencils

Compass

Protractor

Calculator

Folders x 3

Loose leaf, lined binder paper

Correction fluid or tape

Glue stick

Pencil case

Eraser

Highlighter pens

Scissors

Plastic sleeves

Dictionary

Backpack or book bag

USB memory stick

Spiral notebooks (one for
    each subject)

School Planner

organizing and labeling your gear!

common sense doesn't always occur commonly

Okay, so it might sound stupid to even mention this. Might even sound like common sense and you don't need to hear it.

I can even hear you mouthing something that sounds a lot like "Derrrrr!"

But I'll say it anyway… because it's important!

LABEL YOUR STUFF!

Your name is really special — *really* — but I just wish it was on everything you owned. Because, chances are, you're going to lose something — someday or even often. And it's going to sit in a Lost and Found box, alone, if you don't put your name on EVERYTHING!

I'm not saying you have to get a labeling machine or even recruit your entire family into a LABELING FACTORY LINE every summer

> ### tip time
> getting the most out of high school!
>
> *color code your gear. even a dot for one subject can be quite effective when you're in a rush to grab your stuff.*

before school starts. (But if your parents are willing to invest in a labeling device, don't knock it. Besides the ease of processing labels, they can be fun!)

It can be as easy as making up some labels on a computer at home, printing them off in bulk and sticking them on your gear.

There are even some cool online companies that specialize in producing name labels — for everything from your folders to your lunch box. They even make tiny, thin labels that fit perfectly on your pens and pencils. Awesome! Okay, so I *love* labels!

Unfortunately, gear gets lost and stolen at school (by kids less organized than you, of course!), so do yourself a favor and set yourself up for success in this area. It doesn't have to take tons of effort.

Set aside an hour or two (yes, I know, you'll have to put the game console down for at least one level of play).

Put all your school supplies on a large table or clear a space on the floor, naming each and every item. Yes! Even the eraser; just use a pen for that. That way, hopefully, you'll finish the school year with most of your supplies still in your possession.

Another great idea is to color code your gear for each different subject. For example, put red stickers or dots on all your English books, and blue dots or labels on your Math books. That way you can just grab the gear with one particular color before you head off for your lesson. Just be sure to protect your books with paper or a book cover first, otherwise you might get in trouble for turning in a damaged book at the end of the year.

organizing
your folders

divide and conquer

*"Success really starts by becoming master
over the small details of our lives."*

James Rohn

Purchase at least three really big ring binder folders. Girls, you'll especially love this, as most girls love folders and all things stationery! You could go for a color scheme or some other theme. There are tons to choose from these days. Most department stores even stock cool school supplies, as well as stores such as Office Depot, Staples, and other school and office suppliers.

Once you've armed yourself with at least three large ring binders, you're ready to set these up!

Label one of the folders for three or four of your school subjects. For example: English, Social Studies and a language. Use a colored divider for each of these subjects and make sure you put at least ten plastic sleeves behind each divider. That way, you always have one on hand to store any handouts you're given. If you have spiral notebooks for these subjects, pop these in too. Make sure they are named!

tip time

getting the most out of high school!

*notice how the labeling never stops!
for good reason, too!*

For your second folder, you might label this with other subjects, such as Math, Science and Biology, depending on the subjects you are taking. Do the same organizing preparation — dividers and plastic pockets.

Your third folder should be labeled **"Homework Folder."**

We'll discuss how to use it effectively in the homework section of this book, a little later on.

teachers — they're not the enemies!

accounting was the real enemy for me

"Teachers open the door, but you enter by yourself."

Anonymous

I just didn't click with a particular teacher when I was growing up. I didn't like much about her teaching style — a bit gruff and straightforward. And I have to be honest... I wasn't a fan of the subject — "Accounting!"

It was my least favorite subject. The methods confused me and I just couldn't see myself headed that way as a career path. Nothing against accounting — it just wasn't my thing.

Unfortunately, my instructor quickly became my least favorite teacher. And I admit that I didn't respond well either. We even had some fiery conversations in more senior years.

It's not that I didn't really like her as a person. All that mattered to me was that I hated the subject and dreaded my lessons with her.

> ## tip time
> getting the most out of high school!
>
> *look beyond the label on your subject folder, and especially the name tag on your teacher's desk... we're talking about real people!*

Does that sound familiar to your world? Middle school? High school? Well, despite what you may have heard, or what you personally

98

believe, teachers are not your mortal enemies and were not placed on this earth to make your life miserable (although it might seem like that's the case sometimes.)

Teachers are there to guide you through your schooling and to help you learn and discover many things for yourself — not to force feed you tons of useless information that you'll never remember anyway.

As with any relationship, there will be some teachers whose personality you warm to and some you will not. Some teachers will be easier to relate to than others, and basically that's just a part of living within any community.

It's a little like with your extended family — aunts, uncles, and cousins. There are some of your family members who you'll get along with really well. Some others you will just have to learn to tolerate at the least.

Remember that teachers are people too, believe it or not, and they went through high school just the same as you. They really do know what it's like to be a high school student and their job is to help you learn, gain greater independence as a learner, and help you to discover things for yourself.

FORTY

what to do when you don't get along with your teacher

talk it through, with the people who can help

Unfortunately, schools are never ever perfect and not all teachers are perfect either. Sometimes, teachers are just not suited to the difficult task of guiding teenagers. Trust me! It's not an easy job!

If you encounter a difficult teacher, or for some reason you just cannot get along with a teacher, there are some good points you may like to consider to help you through.

Firstly, it's really important that you don't make it personal – even if you feel like the teacher is making it a mission to single you out and make your life a misery! Never make it your personal vendetta to draw other students together against a teacher. Your experience is your experience, and you need to be mature dealing with this issue. I'm not saying to be silent or think it's all your fault all the time. There is just a right and a wrong way of dealing with a teacher/student clash.

> ## tip time
> getting the most out of high school!
>
> *school counselors are often best at dealing with unresolved issues between yourself and a teacher.*

First, try talking to your parents or school counselor. If that doesn't help, or if you feel that it is an important enough issue, seek out a meeting with your school principal. Generally speaking, though, your counselor should be able to offer you valuable guidance and strategies to sort through issues you have with a teacher.

Certainly, a teacher should NEVER put you down in front of students (or by yourself for that matter!). Neither should a teacher intimidate you in any way. Make sure you discuss how you feel with someone whom you trust, if you feel you are being picked on or victimized by a teacher. You may have to be taught by this teacher for a few years so it's best to try to resolve any issues as early as possible. As a word of caution here, don't try to inflame the issue by being rude or disrespectful to the teacher concerned. It just doesn't help either of you.

tips for getting along with your teachers

a bit of eye contact and a listening ear really works

"Nothing is interesting if you're not interested."

Helen MacInness

respect

Show respect for your teachers at all times. You may not always agree with them and you may not always feel like settling down and paying attention in class, but you do need to demonstrate that you can give a basic level of care and respect toward adults.

listen

Listening is a learned skill and one that is very important during your high school years. It is also a sign of respect for your teacher when you listen. Your eye contact will also help demonstrate your attention. You will also miss out on valuable information and instructions if you don't listen.

tip time
getting the most out of high school!

gossip can end with you.

seek further explanation

You will not always understand everything that you see and hear in class. If you are unsure about something or a task that needs to be completed, speak to your teacher about it. Ask the questions.

If the teacher is too busy, ask to arrange a suitable time that you can ask the questions you need for further clarification.

never gossip about your teacher

Spreading gossip means talking about someone behind his or her back. It's all hurtful, no matter what you might think. Live by the rule to never say anything about someone that you wouldn't be comfortable saying to his or her face.

If you hear a rumor or story about a teacher, do not pass it on! It would be better — in a circumstance where you hear some gossip about a teacher — to speak to someone else in authority, such as your class teacher or school counselor. Be the one who puts a stop to such gossip!

Often, how you perceive a teacher is just that — your perception. You see, your emotions relate to how you're feeling about yourself, your stress loads, and what else might be happening in your life at the time.

For example, you might go to school one day after an emotional fight with your mother. Along the way, you realize you've forgotten your English assignment at home. Today is the deadline. And you've already been late once before.

The teacher is not happy. And your response? Well, maybe not so good; angry at yourself more than anyone but you let your tension hit back at the teacher.

You've got someone to blame for your tension now. Mom. The teacher. A series of circumstances that can leave you feeling like no one cares.

The part about Mom can be sorted out at home. You can work it through.

But what about the fallout with the teacher? Do you bother to repair that one? Do you go back later and explain yourself and get the communication channel flowing again?

And, most importantly, do you try to understand where the teacher is coming from? Why there might have been some disciplinary action required from the teacher to teach you and your class a lesson?

Hey, teachers aren't perfect. Neither are moms and dads. Here's the revelation — you're not exactly perfect, either.

"The mediocre teacher tells.
The good teacher explains.
The superior teacher demonstrates.
The great teacher inspires."

William Arthur Ward

"Better to have a variety of teachers and pick
the best from each of them."

James Rohn

"The classroom should be an entrance to the world,
not an escape from it."

John Ciardi

"If you think your teacher is tough,
wait until you get a boss.
He doesn't have tenure."

Bill Gates

"I am indebted to my father for living,
but to my teacher for living well."

Alexander the Great

"A loving, caring teacher took a liking to me.
She noticed potential and wanted to help shape it."

Tom Bradley

"Wise teachers create an environment that
encourages students to teach themselves."

Leonard Roy Frank

"I like the teacher who gives you something to take
home to think about besides homework."

Edith Ann

"The dream begins with a teacher
who believes in you, who tugs and pushes
and leads you to the next plateau,
sometimes poking you with a sharp stick called truth."

Dan Rather
TV Newscaster

"When the student is ready,
the teacher appears."

Anonymous

homework

it's not a dirty word!

I know what you're thinking. Seriously.

The heading contains a two-syllable word. One of those syllables is okay. The other one is a problem.

It starts with w.

Ends with a k.

Put together — not good.

Or... is it?

Homework is actually, seriously, really, NOT a bad word! Okay, so maybe it's not the most pleasant of tasks, and yes, it might just get in the way of your social life — but it's one of the necessary parts of high school. So let's deal with it!

Many students develop the habit of completing homework during their years of elementary school and middle school, but many more don't. So, unfortunately, it becomes one of the major concerns and worries for many teens entering high school.

Try not to stress out! Even if you have secretly *NEVER* completed homework (even though you told your parents and teachers that you did) all hope is not lost! I have come to the rescue, although I may not be wearing a big cape at the moment and a large S for "Super" on the front of my top!

> ## tip time
> getting the most out of high school!
>
> *effective homework time will give you more space in your life for not doing homework*

The good news — the super news in fact — is that some easy homework skills can be learned, practiced, and become a part of your normal life. That'll mean easier completion of your homework tasks and more time to do the things you want to... like stuff that's not homework.

what's the deal with homework?

they're all in there, conspiring!

Ever wondered what happens in the staffroom during break periods and lunch?

Maybe the teachers huddle together and discuss ways to punish and annoy their students. Think so?

Uh, not exactly. Not even close.

Neither is homework a conspiracy to destroy your life! Believe me. It's for your good, whether you know it, like it, or have started laughing right now!

Here are the major reasons why homework is given. I know you won't like to hear them, but please, bear with me...

1. revision

Many of your teachers may give you small homework tasks by way of consolidating (making sure you *really* understand) what has been completed during the day's lesson. You may have heard it said that practice makes perfect. That's really true for many of the methods you might learn for a subject, such as Math, for example.

Just say I have given you a lesson in dental hygiene (brushing and flossing your teeth). I could discuss with you all the various reasons why it's essential that you brush and floss your teeth twice daily. I could then demonstrate for you how to use the toothpaste and which way you should brush your teeth and at which angles. That could be all well and good, but unless you actually complete the task for yourself, and put into practice what you've been taught, you probably won't truly understand the value of the lesson.

Perhaps you've been taught how to write essays in English class. You may be asked to read a list of topics, and then write one short essay for each topic. Now unless you go home and try to write some essays for yourself, in your own time and away from classroom distractions, you may not know if you really understand how to write essays.

So, homework really is, first and foremost, about practice and consolidation.

2. developing study/organizational habits

Another entirely valid reason for homework is that it teaches you, hopefully, to set aside a regular time of day to complete set tasks for school. If done correctly, and you're well prepared, your homework shouldn't take you ages to complete. You will have one or two goals that you might need to complete for homework each night. If you are organized, you should be able to finish them, mark them off your list and then relax for the rest of the evening, guilt free!

"Procrastination is the thief of time."

Edward Young

Procrastination is an ugly word! It means putting off doing something that we know we must do, but we just can't seem to get started on it. We find a million and one other things to do except the very thing that we should be doing. The funny thing is, if we just took the time to complete the task, we'd have it finished in much less time than it's taken us to keep putting it off. (Much like cleaning up your bedroom! *Sound familiar?*)

"Time management is really a misnomer. The challenge is not to manage time, but to manage ourselves."

Steven R Covey

Don't leave your homework tasks hanging over your head like a massive rain cloud. It won't actually go away, even if you pretend it's not there. You'll just have more to complete the next night, and the next, and... you get the picture.

Set yourself a time limit and a goal and get it done! Homework teaches you the valuable lesson of setting a task, then seeing it through to completion. You'll feel a real sense of achievement when you do, and this is a *lifelong skill to develop!*

"The shortest way to do many things
is to do only one thing at once."

Samuel Smiles (1812-1904)

---

3. learning to complete

The third valid reason for homework is that it allows you a set time to complete unfinished tasks from school. Sometimes, you won't finish a piece of work in class due to distractions or lack of understanding. Use 15-20 minutes of your homework time each evening to finish off incomplete school work, if you have any.

how much homework should I do each night?

and why it matters

You'll be discovering in high school that this is a popular question! I guess there is no definitive answer for this question, as every school is different and certainly each grade level has different homework expectations. So the following are merely GUIDELINES — NOT THE FINAL WORD! *(I can just see some of you now quoting this book as a reason you didn't complete that assignment that you've had ALL semester to work on!)*

In your first year of high school, you are certainly not expected to go like a *bull at a gate* and spend five hours at your work station each night, completing pages and pages of homework.

The homework expectations usually increase each year. For freshman year, you might be completing up to an hour and it may increase for the next few years. Usually, in your later school years, particularly your senior year, you'll be expected to complete a couple of hours, or more, each night. This is because you need to complete many more assignments and work requirements, and there is much more studying that needs to be completed for final exams.

Note, what follows is a guideline for completing a small amount each evening. That way it shouldn't build up to an overwhelming state.

A great saying goes like this:

Q. *How do you eat an elephant?*
A. *One bite at a time!*

Imagine you have been given a history assignment on the Industrial Revolution and you have four weeks in which to complete it. Now it would be very easy to see this assignment as a giant elephant — the task just seems so HUGE and overwhelming.

If you break it down into smaller, more bite-sized chunks, however, completing this mammoth task can become quite manageable.

Let's map it out:

week 1

List six major questions that you will research.
Borrow library books
Begin reading and taking notes

113

week 2

Write down notes under each of the six major research questions.
Complete research notes by the end of the second week.
Type up Bibliography page, listing all the sources you used.

week 3

Collect diagrams and pictures that you'll use for your project.
Write up rough draft of assignment.
Ask your parent or guardian to proofread the rough draft
and check for spelling and grammatical errors.

week 4

Type up the final copy of your assignment. Make sure you take
note of any changes made by your proofreader.
Add in illustrations and pictures.
Design front cover
Submit your assignment!

PS: Make sure you thank your "proofreader"/parent/guardian... they'll appreciate your gratefulness and might even be willing to help out next time!

"Motivation is what gets you started.
Habit is what keeps you going."
Jim Ryun

"The best way to get something done is to begin."
Unknown

"No one knows what he can do until he tries."
Latin proverb

"The shortest way to do many things is to
do only one thing at once."
Samuel Smiles

"Perhaps the most valuable result of all education is the ability
to make yourself do the thing you have to do, when it ought to
be done, whether you like it or not; it is the first lesson that
ought to be learned; and however a person's training begins,
it is probably the last lesson they learn thoroughly."
Thomas H. Huxley (1825-1895)

"Don't be afraid to give your best to what seemingly are
small jobs. Every time you conquer one it makes you that
much stronger. If you do the little jobs well, the big ones
will tend to take care of themselves."
Dale Carnegie

"Laziness may appear attractive, but work gives satisfaction."
Anne Frank

invalid homework
excuses

the stuff that won't fly with teachers. believe me.

"I had to clean my room."

"We had visitors."

"I forgot!"

"I left my gear at school."

"The dog chewed it up and now I have to wait for it to come out!"

"We were visited by aliens and all they took back with them was
my homework!"

"I thought it was due next week."

"I couldn't find a pen."

"My mom threw it out."

"It got wet."

"We used it to start our fire."

"I left it in the car."

"It's on my desk at home."

"I squashed my banana on it accidentally."

"It got washed out to sea at a family beach trip last night."

"My little sister ripped it up."

"I didn't have any paper."

"My mom wouldn't let me."

"My grandma came to stay."

"I was too busy reading a book by Sharon Witt!" (Note from
the author: I like your reading taste, but it's a bad
homework excuse!)

and the worst of all would be…

"I dunno."

creating a
homework space

preferably better than this principal's office!

Imagine that you had an appointment in your principal's office one day to discuss an issue.

When you arrive at her office, you find wall-to-wall papers lying everywhere, folders lying open all over the floor and bits and pieces of what appear to be junk and candy wrappers across the desktop!

"Wait a minute," she says. "I can't find my glasses!"

You look away, laughing in secret. Not only are the glasses on her head but she's also forgotten to replace her pajamas with something more professional for the day's appointments.

What's wrong with this story?

Well, it's just not going to happen. It's not reality.

Most principals will be ordered. Well prepared. And their work space will be something more ordered than the fiction we joked about above.

Now, to give yourself every chance of success, you need to set up a properly organized work station or student office.

This doesn't need to be an expensive exercise. All you really need is a good sturdy table and a chair. We'll cover some of the other essentials a little later.

The space must be just for you, so that you have somewhere to go each night for a set time. You may only have your bedroom available. If you choose your room, try to make it as uncluttered as possible. It is also advisable not to have a TV in the same place as you study because it can be a huge distraction. A section of the family room can also be just as valuable or if you're really lucky you might even have a separate study at home that you can use.

"A place for everything, and everything in its place."

Samuel Smiles (1812-1904)

Once you've decided on a suitable location, you'll need to make sure that you set up your homework space for maximum effect — you need to ensure success, so it's no use having a table and chair with no equipment. Try to imagine you are setting up a work office. Now you can have some fun. You might want to choose a particular color theme (oooooh! I hear the girls scream). Basically, you'll need the following equipment at your work station so you'll be properly prepared.

homework station equipment

Spare paper/lined paper
Pens and pencils
Dictionary
Atlas
Whiteboard or corkboard
Eraser and whiteout
Plastic pockets
Large folder — homework
Calculator
Computer (desirable, but not necessarily essential)

top homework tips!

- Set aside a specific, designated area that you will be able to complete homework at each night.

- Ensure you have the right tools you'll need.

- Establish a routine: Try to stick to the same time each night – routine soon becomes habit!

- Keep it simple! Try to complete simple and reasonable small homework tasks on the day they are set for each subject. That way, they won't build up and you are less likely to forget to complete them.

- Homework Folder. Use a homework folder to carry work to and from school. That way, you won't have to lug home ten folders and 50 textbooks. (There's more detail about this in the next chapter.)

- Don't procrastinate! Putting off work that needs to be done is the ultimate time waster – it just stresses you out anyway, so just sit down and get it done!

setting up a
homework folder

one folder to rule them all!

This is a really cool idea and one that I find helps many students organize their homework for ultimate success. You can use any type of ring binder or ordinary folder. It doesn't have to be a large, bulky one. Label it clearly as **"Homework Folder."** Inside this folder, add about 10-15 plastic pockets. You may even like to go one step further and add individual subject dividers for each of the subjects you'll have homework assigned for. Make sure you also include loose leaf, lined paper in the folder to complete assignments.

As you receive handouts or worksheets for homework, you can then simply pop these into the plastic pockets. If you have reasonably thin textbooks you can actually slide these in the plastic sleeves as well. This way, you really only need to take home your homework folder from school each day. When you've completed a piece of homework, place this

tip time
getting the most out of high school!

make a spot for notices in your homework folder.

then your one folder becomes a "one-stop shop" for after-school work.

into a plastic sleeve inside your folder so you won't misplace it before your next lesson.

notices

Go one step further and clearly label one of the plastic pockets as "**Notices.**" This way, all your school notices can be placed in the same folder that goes home each day. Hopefully, the notices will then make it home safely to Mom and Dad.

tests and exams

sitting for tests while standing on solid ground

You may be tested from time to time by some teachers to gauge your level of understanding of different subjects. This assists your teachers in knowing what you have remembered and areas you may need to improve on.

It also helps the teacher to make the lessons productive and effective.

You're most likely to receive regular testing in the areas of Math, Science and English.

You shouldn't be too stressed out about exams in high school. While it's true that you do need to study for them and ensure you are well prepared, your results are not the 'be-all-and-end-all' assessment of your abilities. If your marks are not high, it does not mean you will automatically repeat the school year. Schools take many factors into consideration before recommending a student to repeat a year.

Once you move into the latter years of high school — there is certainly a greater emphasis placed on final exam results. And students hoping to get into a good college will need to get good grades even in high school.

Special tests such as the SAT or ACT are usually given to help determine how much you *really* learned in school. These tests are part of the package asked for by most colleges and universities.

Exam time can be very stressful for many students. It doesn't have to be! There are many useful tips and advice that can help you prepare well for your exams and to deal with stress when you're feeling overwhelmed.

study tips for exams

routine

Set a regular timeframe in which to study each night and stick to it. It's important that your study time becomes a habit.

study space

It's really important that your study space is both comfortable and well lit. Don't sit on the couch or on your bed to study. Sit at a desk where your study time is purposeful.

establish a schedule

When you are studying for a series of tests or exams, it's helpful to draw up a study schedule to ensure that you dedicate specific time for each subject.

look after your health

It's difficult to study on an empty stomach or when you have no energy. Make sure you drink lots of water; try to avoid too many caffeinated drinks, such as coffee and Coke. Have lots of healthy snacks on hand (nuts are a great source of energy) and exercise regularly. Take short breaks at specific times during your study schedule. Go for a walk or do some other physical activity.

sleep

You won't retain any information if you are dog tired, so if it's late or you are just plain exhausted, go to bed! You can always set your alarm and get up early in the morning to catch up.

avoid interruptions

When you are in study mode, try to avoid things like having the computer and internet on (social networking sites are killer time-wasters!). That'll protect you from being distracted by messages constantly popping up. The same goes for your cell phone — make sure it is switched off when you are studying or out of the room.

Let your family know your study schedule (post a copy on the fridge) and ask them not to disturb you during your study periods if possible.

be calm!

There isn't a great deal of purpose to be had for stressing yourself out! You can only do what you can do, so the best cure for stress is to do something about what's stressing you. That just might be preparing for your exams. When you need to take a break, try lying down somewhere peaceful and listening to some calming music. Let the music take you away.

tip time

getting the most out of high school!

routine study makes all the difference.

set rewards

As with any goals, set yourself some mini rewards for when you take study breaks. For example, watch a TV show, catch up with friends, play a sport, or watch your favorite movie.

ask for help

If you are unsure about any part of your subject matter, make sure you seek out your teacher and *ask* for clarification — that's what your teachers are there for! Another great help can be from your peers. Ask a classmate for help if you're struggling. You can always repay the favor by offering to help them in another subject.

find a study partner

A study partner *can* be really helpful if you're studying for a subject that isn't your strength. Two heads can often be better than one if you're trying to understand a problem or concept. A word of warning here, though — you have to be really strict with yourself if you are going to be study partners. It can be easy to get distracted by chatting about other stuff when you're together. A study partner might be best used for one or two subjects.

try study assistance

Peer tutoring can be one of the most beneficial ways to understand parts of a subject that you're struggling with. Often, when a friend or classmate explains something in your own language, you will understand it better. Try finding a classmate, or perhaps an older student, who can offer you help in studying. If you are really great at English, for example, you could then offer to help someone else who struggles with this subject area.

The added bonus of peer tutoring is that, often, helping someone else helps cement your own knowledge and understanding because you are having to explain it to someone else.

exam tips

first things first...look after yourself

You won't be able to perform at your best if you haven't fueled your body properly. If your exam is in the morning, make sure you've had a good, healthy breakfast. Ensure you have had a good snack before your exam — fruit, for example — and bring a bottle of water to stay hydrated during your test.

getting closer...get a good night's sleep

The night before your exams, make sure you get a good night's sleep! You've studied all you can (hopefully). Even if you haven't, the night before won't make too much difference, so there's nothing left to do but get a good, solid night's rest. Your brain will thank you for it in the morning!

when you get to the exam...read the entire exam paper first

There was a funny joke played on students once (not during exams though!) in which the teacher instructed students to read the entire test paper first before beginning. Clearly, not all students did as asked, as many spent the entire hour of their test busily concentrating and writing. Those that did read the entire test first actually finished in about five minutes flat and sat there smiling, looking very satisfied with themselves. Why? Because the very last question on the test paper said, "Ignore all other questions and complete only number 1!"

Once you've read all the exam questions, without delay,

you can then plan how much time you should allocate to each question and section of the exam.

complete all questions

This might sound obvious, but many students simply leave a question if they don't know the answer. Even if you are unsure, you should at least give the question a go. One point or even half a point received can be the difference between a pass and a fail.

be prepared!

Make sure you arrive at your exam with the appropriate equipment! You will need at least two pens — an extra one in case a pen runs out — pencil, calculator, and eraser. You can't ask someone for a pen midway through your exam!

plan your exam time

As soon as you have read carefully through your exam, write a quick exam schedule on a piece of scrap paper so that you can allocate a set amount of time for each section. This will help ensure that you don't leave yourself short on time for completing the final section.

why do I need to know all this stuff?

This is a fairly common question among students. "Why do I need to know all this information and subject matter at school?" I know when I was studying 11th grade Accounting, that's precisely what I was thinking.

"I'll never even use this stuff anyway," I told my teacher. Well guess what!? Now, 20 years later, I'm running my own publishing business and I am doing all my own accounts! So you just never know when or where you'll draw on some of this knowledge.

True, you won't remember a lot of what you'll learn in high school. But remember, it's not just **what** you learn; it's the process of **being** a learner. Learning skills such as listening, comprehension, writing, discussing, and study habits are all valuable skills that you'll use once you've completed your high school education.

PART 4

A+

help is
at hand

I don't get it!

struggling with subjects

"Nothing is interesting if you're not interested."

Helen MacInness

Sometimes, you will have trouble understanding a subject.

The truth is, some areas of school just seem to suit us better than others. I really struggled with Math and Accounting during high school. I just didn't get it! It may have been partly due to the explanations used by my teachers, but it was also because I often tuned out when things got difficult. It was like going off to Disneyland in my mind! I was in a whole other world. This is NOT helpful, of course. Tuning out is not a great response to lack of understanding.

ask for help!

I *never* understood fractions in Math. I just never got it! The explanations offered to me by my Math teachers just added to my confused state. It wasn't long before I was a teacher myself, and guess what subject I was given in my first year of teaching? You guessed it... Math.

By then, I was forced to actually ask a fellow teacher to explain to me how fractions worked. BINGO! I understood his explanation immediately. *"Is that all?"* I asked.

So, sometimes it might require a teacher to explain it to you, one-on-one, or another student to have a shot, before the penny drops and *you* understand the concepts! The point is, don't be afraid to ask. You should never get in trouble for asking for help!

when high school isn't working for you

thinking through the reasons

It is true that high school doesn't work out for everyone. It could be for a variety of reasons — lack of stimulating programs; inability to concentrate; your individual learning style might clash. There could be a whole host of reasons.

Some students will struggle through the years of high school before they finally leave and gain work or start an internship. It's a legal requirement to attend high school, so if it's not working too well for you, this can really make life difficult until you can legally depart.

tip time
getting the most out of high school!

***talk to someone
about how you feel.***

attendance

This may seem a really obvious point to make if you are reading this, but it must be said. You actually ***need*** to attend high school! Not only is it a legal requirement that you attend school, but you need to attend in order to give yourself the very best chance of being successful. Many teachers have explained that one of the biggest factors in a student's success at high school is whether he or she turns up or not!

You see, if you get into the habit of taking regular days off, you actually miss important pieces of information and instructions that are often difficult to catch up on secondhand. Sure, there will be times when it's just not possible to attend school; for example, if you are ill or there are other major problems. Taking regular days off, however, because you don't feel up to it (or you're exhausted because you've been staying up late watching TV), will not cut it in the long run.

You only need to miss a couple of days to get yourself behind. If you can possibly help it, make sure you at least turn up to school, even when you just don't feel like it. If you do happen to miss a day, it is your responsibility to seek out the teachers you missed seeing, and find out about any work missed and homework that needs to be completed. Sometimes, you can miss a few days and then get stuck in a rut because you fall further and further behind. That's not helpful for you.

Your best chance of success at high school is to make sure you attend!

In any case, if you've got issues with just being at school, consider these important pieces of advice and guidance...

attitude

Sometimes, how we are feeling about a situation actually comes down to our attitude. It may be more about what we are saying to ourselves about each situation, and the negative language and explanations we use for our life at the moment.

For example, each time you go to a science class, you might say to yourself, "I hate Science" or "It's the most boring subject in the world!" Well, guess what? You will probably find that lesson incredibly boring, given your preset attitude.

Instead, try this. Next time you go to a science class, try saying to yourself, "I really find it difficult to understand science sometimes, but today I'm going to really try to concentrate and ask as many questions as I can. I'm going to participate in this class as if it were my last science lesson." You know what? You just might come away feeling a lot more positive about that lesson than you would have otherwise. You have nothing to lose!

I often hear students saying comments like "School sucks" or "I really hate Math."

You will create your **own** reality by your thoughts and behaviors – you really will. When you are in a negative frame of mind, it can't help but affect what then occurs. I can't emphasize enough how important it is that you try to remain positive. Try to fake it 'til you make it! In other words, pretend you actually like school until things turn around!

peer groups

Sometimes, students don't enjoy their high school experience because of peer groups or lack of friends. This can be really difficult. For many teens, friendship and peer groups rate as one of the most important reasons for enjoying high school. So if this area isn't working too well for you, then it goes without saying that school might feel pretty ordinary. The best advice here is to get out there and try to make friends. You might say, "Well, I've already tried that and it's just not working for me. I have NO friends." Okay, well that may be your present circumstance. That might be what you're feeling right now, but there are things you can do to try to change this. Have you tried joining a group or club within the high school?

For example, you could try joining the student council or leadership group, the school band, choir, debate team, or one of the many sports teams. The list is pretty endless, but the point is, that's where a lot of new friendships are formed.

When I run a student council group with high school students, the comment I most often hear is that students discover new people they would never have known otherwise. New friendships and social groupings can often be born out of joining a school club, so don't write that avenue off!

communicate

If you try some of the above strategies and are still feeling like school is just not working for you, it's important that you share your concerns with someone. That might be your school counselor, your parents, or a church youth worker. Sometimes, a wise adult can give us some further strategies to consider that we might not have thought of before. The most important point is that you need to talk about it. There might be a number of options out there for you to consider. Remember, you are not the only one who has been challenged to like school, and you won't be the last!

I want to change schools!

big decisions mean big thinking. let's not be hasty

Sometimes, for a whole bunch of reasons, the high school that you attend may just not be working for you at the moment.

Maybe you have tried and are just not able to form friendship groups. Perhaps the school is just not the right one for you.

Now, I'm not saying that you should hound your parents to change schools at the first hint of not liking the place where you are. I'm not saying that at all. Because, for many students, there will be some point at which you just aren't enjoying your high school experience. For most, though, these feelings soon pass.

But for a small minority of students, their chosen high schools just don't seem to fit, no matter how much they try. In some circumstances, a student might need to make a change or a fresh start at a new high school. This shouldn't be taken as a light decision, but one that is made with the full support of your parents.

If this is you right now, and you really hate your high school environment, there are a few steps you ought to take.

Firstly, talk to your parents about how you are feeling. Pick a suitable time though, not right in the middle of the nightly television newscast or when a parent just walks in the door from a long day at work. Ask your parents when would be the best time to have a chat. It might even help if you write a few bullet points down first on a piece of paper. If you are really serious about changing schools, it would be helpful to have some clear reasons to share with your parents.

Talking to your school counselor would also be a positive step. Even if you do end up leaving the school, there might be some valuable advice they could pass on to you.

It's not always a bad thing to change schools. When I was halfway through high school, my parents moved me to another high school which they felt met my educational needs better *(basically it was a much stricter academic school and I needed a big kick in my tush!)*. Even though it was not my choice at the time, my parents really did know what was best for me and the move to another school was very beneficial.

a conclusion for me...
a beginning for you

Thanks for taking the time to read *Surviving High School.*

My hope for you is that you won't just survive high school, but that you'll thrive! High school can be just what you decide to make it. You can let it be a fantastic and amazing stage of your life and just embrace all the changes that it brings. And even though you might go through some bumpy patches and challenges and growth, remember this — high school won't last forever and hopefully you'll come through the end of it with some great memories!

contact Sharon:

Sharon Witt

Email: sharon@sharonwitt.com.au

Website: www.sharonwitt.com.au

Mail: Collective Wisdom Publications

PO Box 150, Mt Evelyn Victoria 3796, Australia

About the author:

Sharon Witt is a devoted wife, fulfilled mom, prolific writer, guest speaker, dedicated teacher, former television actress, and more! When she's not waiting for Oprah Winfrey to invite her for an interview, Sharon Witt is a high school coordinator in Mt Evelyn Christian School on the outskirts of Melbourne, Australia. She has worked extensively with students as a teacher, mentor, and counselor.